A is for Aloha

Stephanie Feeney

with photographs by Hella Hammid

designed by Einar Vinje

A Kolowalu Book
University of Hawaii Press
Honolulu

About the book

A is for Aloha uses the ABC book format to portray some of the people, places, and experiences that make up the everyday life of children in Hawaii. We created it so that Hawaii's young children could have a book showing familiar experiences to which they could relate. We also wanted children in other places to have a glimpse of what life is like on our beautiful islands and to convey the spirit of aloha to people everywhere.

We wish to acknowledge the wonderful children who were the subjects of these photographs, the preschool teachers and directors who were so helpful and generous with their time, and the parents who allowed us to use their children's pictures in this book. Our thanks to the children and staff of the Family Services Center, Flamingo School, the Early School, Diamond Head Child Care Center, St. Timothy's Children's Center, and the Kindergarten and Children's Aid Association's Kula Kamalii School. We are especially grateful to Steve Albert and the teachers and children at Rainbow School for their invaluable assistance, and to Jackie Dudock for her participation in all aspects of this project. Thanks also to Diane Sheets for her help in setting up photographic sites, and to Eva Moravcik, Fred Braun, Kelvin Young for their suggestions.

We hope that you will enjoy this photographic celebration of childhood in Hawaii and that it will provide special moments of sharing for you and your children.

Stephanie Feeney

A a
aloha

B b

baby
beach
ball

C c
canoe

Ee
eat

F f

friend

G g
gecko

Hh

hair
hibiscus

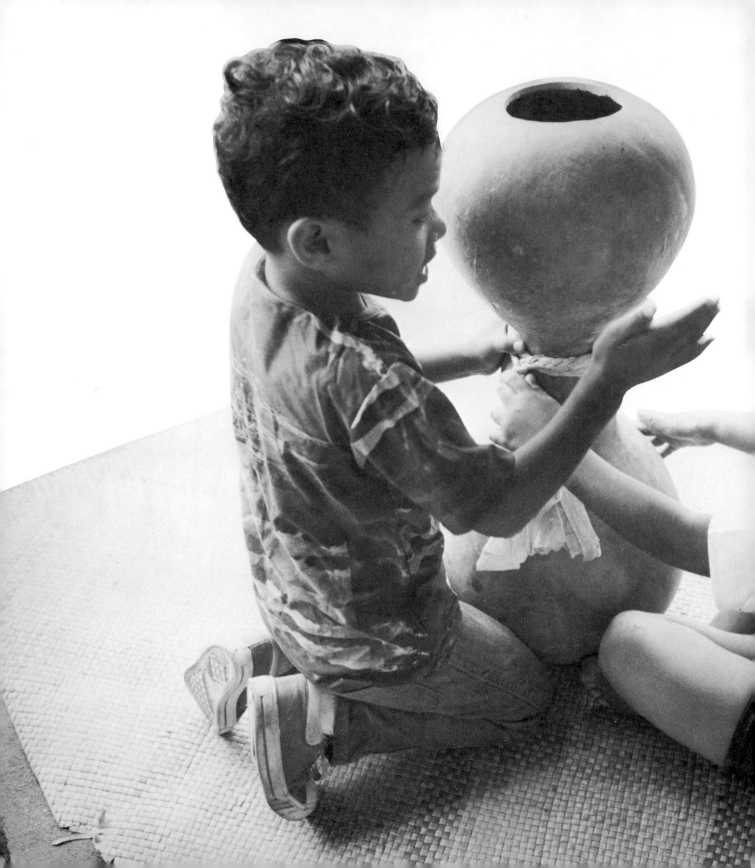

I i

ipu

J j

jump

Kk

kiss

Ll

lei

M m
Mommy
muumuu

N n
net

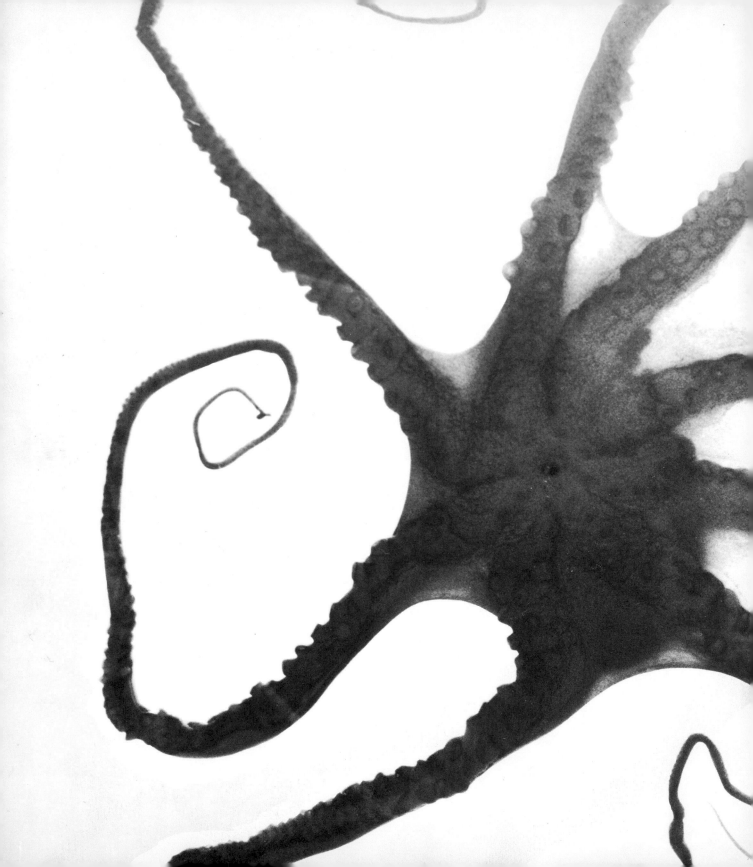

Oo

octopus

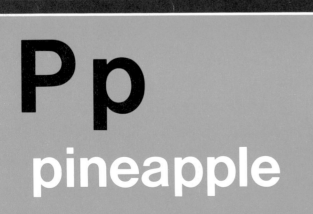

Pp
pineapple

Qq

quilt

R r

rain

S s sand
sea
shell

Tt
Tutu

U u

ukulele

V v
volcano

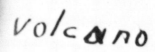

Lars

volcano

W w

waterfall

X x

x-ing

Yy

yucky

Z z
zoris

About Hawaii

The State of Hawaii is composed of a chain of islands in the Pacific Ocean. It is very different from the rest of the United States, which is referred to in Hawaii as the *mainland.* The weather is warm all year long, the sky is very blue, the ocean is almost turquoise blue in places and so clear that you can see the coral reefs and tropical fish. There are many green mountains that were once volcanoes but that no longer erupt, and there are two active volcanoes on the biggest island, which is called Hawaii. There are many kinds of palm trees, lush tropical plants, and brightly colored flowers that bloom all year. Lizards, many kinds of birds, and mongooses live in Hawaii, but there are no snakes or squirrels. Often it rains when the sun is shining and then we see beautiful rainbows.

The first settlers of the Hawaiian Islands were Polynesians who came by canoe from other far-distant islands in the Pacific. Many years later missionaries and whalers came from the eastern United States. Europeans came to trade, and later, people from Asia and the Pacific, including Japanese, Chinese, Filipinos, Koreans, and Samoans, came to work and live in Hawaii. The people who came to Hawaii from all of these places brought many kinds of plants, animals, arts and crafts, and household items with them. Hawaii is an interesting and colorful place to live because there is a combination of so many peoples and cultures.

The lives of children in Hawaii are in many ways like the lives of children on the mainland. They live in houses or apartments in the city (the biggest is the city of Honolulu on the island of Oahu) or in the country. They get from place to place on their island by car and bus and between islands by plane. Children live with their mothers and fathers and sometimes with their grandparents (called tutus by most island children) and other relatives. Most people in Hawaii speak English, but many also speak a rhythmic, shortened form of English called pidgin, which includes words from other languages.

Children in Hawaii like to do the things that children do everywhere. They go to school, play with their friends, help at home, listen to stories, and watch television. Because it is usually warm and sunny and it is easy to get to the beach when you live on an island, children enjoy many water activities. They like to swim, dig in the sand and build sand castles, go fishing with their families, and sometimes even go for a ride on a surfboard.

Most of the time children wear only shorts, T-shirts, and rubber thongs called zoris. In many homes it is not considered polite to wear your shoes in the house, and most people leave them by the door before they go inside. Girls sometimes wear long, brightly colored dresses called muumuus. Children in Hawaii never need snowsuits, mittens, or heavy boots because it is never cold enough to snow, except at the top of the tallest mountains.

Foods that children on the mainland like—hamburgers, hot dogs, milk, and ice cream—are also popular with Hawaiian children. They also like a noodle soup called *saimin,* and shave ice—cones of crushed ice with flavored syrup. In Hawaii children also eat Chinese, Japanese, and Hawaiian foods and many kinds of tropical fruits, such as pineapples, papayas,

mangoes, and coconuts. People in Hawaii eat lots of rice. A scoop of rice is sometimes eaten with eggs for breakfast.

The holidays of Halloween, Thanksgiving, Christmas, Valentine's Day, and Easter are celebrated in Hawaii, as they are on the mainland. Other holidays were introduced from other places. Chinese New Year is honored by firecrackers and a special dance called a "lion dance." Japanese Boy's Day is celebrated by hanging fish banners, and Girl's Day with the display of beautiful Japanese dolls. The birthdays of Prince Kuhio and King Kamehameha are state holidays in Hawaii, and May Day, called Lei Day, is a time for wearing flower necklaces and singing songs and dancing dances from the cultures of Hawaii.

Another thing that makes Hawaii different from the rest of the United States is that it is the only state that once had kings and queens. Hawaii has a government like other states now, but people still have fond memories of the days of the royalty. Beautiful songs written about the kings and queens of Hawaii are still sung and the much-loved song, *Aloha Oe,* was written by Hawaii's last queen, Liliuokalani.

If you want to learn more, look in your local library for books about the history, geography, and cultures of Hawaii.

About the words

ALOHA

A Hawaiian word that conveys warm feelings and can be used to say "hello," "goodbye," and "I love you."

CANOE

A narrow, light boat moved with paddles. Ancient Hawaiians traveled between islands in canoes fitted with outriggers. An outrigger is a wooden support on the side to prevent the canoe from tipping. Racing outrigger canoes is still a popular sport in Hawaii.

GECKO

A small gray lizard with a large head, short body, and suction pads on its feet. A gecko makes a strange chirping noise. Geckos are found in most homes in Hawaii where they are welcomed because they eat insects.

HIBISCUS

A very common shrub in Hawaii that has large, brilliantly colored flowers. Hibiscus is the Hawaii state flower.

IPU

(Pronounced *ee-poo.*) A rhythm instrument made from a hollow gourd which is used to accompany Hawaiian chants and the hula.

LEI

(Pronounced *lay.*) A Hawaiian word for the necklace of flowers, leaves, or shells given with a kiss to show affection or appreciation.

MUUMUU

(Pronounced *moo-oo moo-oo.*) A long, loose fitting dress, usually brightly patterned, which was introduced by the missionaries. The muumuu is well suited to Hawaii's warm climate.

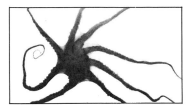

OCTOPUS

A large-headed, soft-bodied ocean dweller that has eight arms covered with suckers. Octopus is caught by spear on the coral reefs and is used for food.

PINEAPPLE

A tropical plant with a juicy, yellow fruit that looks like a very big pine cone. Originally brought from South America, pineapple is now one of Hawaii's major crops.

QUILT

Hawaiians created their own kind of decorative bedcover based on those introduced by the missionaries. Hawaiian quilts usually have only two colors, and the patterns are taken from island flowers and plants.

TUTU

The Hawaiian word for grandmother or grandfather.

UKULELE

(Pronounced *oo-koo-lay-lay.*) A small, usually four-stringed guitar, which was introduced by the Portuguese and is now a popular Hawaiian instrument.

VOLCANO

An opening in the earth's surface, sometimes shaped like a mountain, from which molten rock called lava erupts. Hawaii's mountains were once volcanoes and most of the land on the islands is formed from lava rock.

ZORIS

A Japanese word for sandals with thongs and open backs that are popular in Hawaii. Children generally call them "slippers."

Sharing this book with children

A is for Aloha can be used to stimulate language and to help children develop interest in reading and in learning more about Hawaii. Begin by looking at the pictures with your child, talk about what each of you sees, and share your feelings and reactions with each other. If the child seems interested in learning more you can read and discuss the information in the sections about Hawaii and about the words.

Practice in letter recognition, important in the beginning reading process, can be encouraged as the child learns to recognize the similarities between the alphabet letters and the same letter in the word describing the picture. Learning the names of the letters of the alphabet does not help in reading because the child needs to understand that letters make up words and are meaningful only in the context of the word. It is better for a child to learn the sounds for the letters than to memorize the alphabet.

You can help your child learn the sounds by pointing to the letter D, for example, making the sound for D, and then saying the word Daddy emphasizing the initial sound. You can then talk about other words that begin with the same sound. In general, it is best to begin with consonant sounds. The Hawaiian vowels used in some of the words in this book are different from standard English vowel sounds, and it would be best not to use them to teach vowel sounds.

Sharing a picture book with a child can be a very special experience, and is one of the best ways to help the child to develop an interest in books and in reading. We hope this book will be a source of enjoyment for you and your child.

Author: Stephanie Feeney is professor of education at the University of Hawaii, where she has developed the early childhood education program and taught since 1972. She also serves as a consultant for preschool programs on Oahu and the neighbor islands. *A is for Aloha* grew out of her concern that so little material was available in these schools that was relevant to the lives of children in Hawaii. Dr. Feeney received her education at UCLA, Harvard, and Claremont Graduate School. Prior to teaching in Hawaii, she was a teacher, social worker, and education specialist. She is coauthor of *Who Am I in the Lives of Children?,* an introduction to teaching young children, and author of *Hawaii is a Rainbow.*

Photographer: Hella Hammid was born in Germany and educated in France, England, and the United States. She has been a freelance photographer for *Life Magazine, Town and Country, The New York Times,* and the *Los Angeles Times.* She has taught photography at UCLA, and has had many exhibitions of her work. She is represented in major collections, including that of the Museum of Modern Art. Hammid's photographs of children appear in *The Sensible Book* and *Teaching Your Wings to Fly.* Her work also appears in the *Family of Man,* in other books, and on children's record album covers.

Designer: Einar Vinje was trained in design in Norway and Canada, and currently has his design studio in San Francisco. He has been publications art director at McGill University and has designed books, magazines, and company literature for Sunset Books, Saul Bass, Reader's Digest Press, Prentice-Hall, Eastern Airlines, San Francisco Magazine, Crocker Bank, and many others. Vinje is concerned with the harmony between the concept and the design, and his distinctive, bold style has resulted in a number of design awards.